If You Read Me,

Don't Fall in Love

by Flumaer.

If You Read Me, Don't Fall in Love

For little me,
who always dreamed of being a published writer.

Content

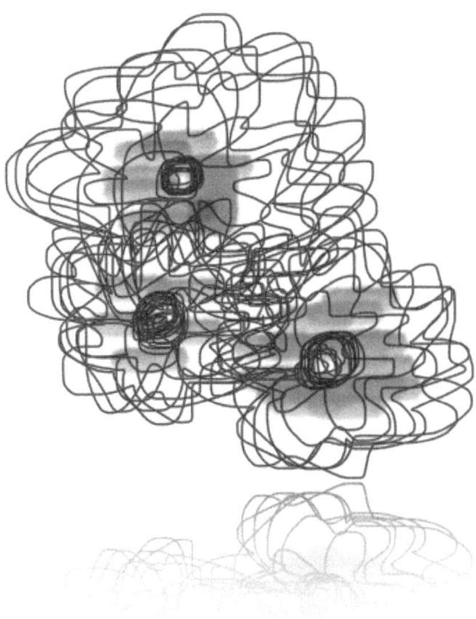

SHE

IS

GODDESS.

she ain't looking for love.
she is love.

confide in me,
trust me once —
for you I will banish sorrow from fate.

every night moon doesn't set,
it bows—
just to brush against her feet.

she wears her aching like those emerald
and Goddamn—
does she not look flawlessly
breathtaking.

she doesn't need words
to define her beauty
she is Winter,
thunder,
fire,

— everything a poet desires for in their poetry.

heaven was never real to me
until her lips curved into light.

now I know —
heaven is nothing but her
& her
& only her.

she isn't poem,
she is the solace, poets kneels before.

how could someone not love her—
in her veins runs loyalty
& her soul carries kindness.

my typewriter turns to poetry when I write about her,
she is beyond words, beyond the world—
every alphabet I place becomes a note,
& together, they rise into symphony.

to be loved by her is blessing—
her veins carry the heat of storms,
the soul burns with a fire that refuses to dim.

she doesn't just exist—
she reshapes the world around her
leaving spark in her wake,
& a quiet reckoning in every heartbeat she touches.

i carved temples into my skin for him while he worshipped somewhere else.

she is not a name, not a face,
but a tide that rises inside your chest.

to love her is to drown willingly,
to surrender to the current of flaws.

without her, I am hollow.
it is her love connecting my neurones,
her world in which I stumble,
it is her gravity that keeps me alive.

her chaos was tide.
her sanity a shore.

in both she loved me—
once wild, once gently,

always entirely.

she loves me,
& i float beyond the reach of gravity.

i wandered through every place that promised calm—
waterfall, moonlight, the edge of death.

yet, only in her arms did i rest.

I am the light your heart chase,
the darkness your soul craves.

and a single look from you
was enough to alter my world;

to pull starts from the sky & to carve you
into lines of my palm.

//you, you were game changer.

her eyes met mine.

suddenly, the world aligned—
nothing else mattered.

you travel countries to find love;
crossing ocean, chasing hearts

& still it was her gaze all along.
GODDAMN, the entire world lived there.

they talk about love,
i talk about you.

with her, I dream of the '80s.

i breathe decade of summers and then sink into her.

her voice cracks mountains,
her silence moves oceans.

I exist only because she allows it.

while I was never brave enough,
she gave me strength.

the darkness I carried,
my pain,
my sorrow,
she found them all
& laid
        them
            to
                rest.

let her touch you,
this one time.

let her wander
in the darkness
of your mind & bring light.

i trace the curve of her neck,
the line of her shoulder
& hunger rises in me—

but she only smiles,
as if she knows the power she holds.

SHE

IS

WARRIOR.

Warrior isn't glory—
it's the girl who would not stay buried.

an afraid soul, always
but she carried herself like a hurricane—

grateful, unyeilding, unstoppable.

you can't tame fire, when it was born to burn.

you can't hunt the witches and dream about putting an
end to magic;
'cause it is everywhere—

it runs in my veins,
it rests in my bones
& blazes in the air that dares to hold me.

my body is battlefield
& my skin remembers each scar.

how ironic— she was taught to bow,

yet she learned to
break
the
altar.

i remember the world mocking me,
laughing at my fragility;

until I showed them
how to break glass with bare hands.

i have this habit of tracing my scars,

as if my fingers could chart their lines &
carry me back to the night
i refused
to
die.

you must see her—
even in defeated battle,
her bones hums like drum
beating for war victory.

how could a woman carry a sword?

how could she fight with grace when her own stood against?

so, she learned—
to wield world sharpened by wisdom.

the war is finally over!!

and she, still wearing her armour.

i dream about the peaceful nights

but the fists never unclench.

oh, look at her—
shaking, terrified !!

and still taking the next step.

they see the armour.

they never see the trembling hands.

she was something else.
no god crowned her.
they tried to tame her fire—

yet she rose, dirt in her mouth, fire in her eyes.

she is the woman who claws through battles
and still kisses like mercy.

my rage is holy—
every tear I shed, an offering.

i am
a daughter of ruins.
what you should fear in me is—

survival.

i kissed my scars—
again,
again—
until they forgave me.

she had fallen
two many times
and every time she did,
the earth
remembered her shape.

she glowed,

through arrow holes
they swore
would end her.

i carry the wars
that ended
before I was born.

still
i walk.

she stitched herself back
with thread of rage—

and it almost
looked like love.

SHE

IS

HUMAN

she moves through the room
like a soft melody
no one dares to echo.

her skin glimmers,
her step flows,
her gaze fixed beyond the walls.

you can watch her,
but never arrive.

her desire belongs to her alone.

your hands hold nothing—
just the silence
she drifts through.

i'm still learning
where yielding ends and vanishing begins.

some nights I give myself away
and wake a stranger
wearing my own skin.

i chose peace,
but grieved it like death.

i buy cheap flowers
just to watch them outlive my last romance.

somehow it's a comfort,
seeing something fade slower than I did.

i just wanted someone to hold me forever,
but no one ever cared enough to notice–

so, I kept my mouth shut.

fear walks beside me.
so does hunger—

not only for food,
but to chase dreams, find love,

to get a life
i'm allowed to want.

mistakes stick to me like perfume.

i smell them before I walk in.
still, I walk in.

loneliness is my longest lover.

we share coffee,
split cigarettes,
argue over who's leaving first.

i keep my scars private
not because i'm ashamed
but because they're mine.

even my pain deserves boundaries.

i still write letters
to no one's hands.

the ink spreads slowly,
like my heart spilling secrets
it can't afford to tell.

i fold the paper carefully—
a ritual of order
to tame what refuses
to be tamed.

i have a wild laugh
and a quiet grief.

both fit inside me
like lungs.

In and out.
Constant.

lipstick like armor.

a shield i smear away
on my sleeve
before leaning into a kiss
that shouldn't happen.

still, the sweetness lingers—

guilt dressed in sugar
on my lips,
a flavour I know
i'll crave again.

in my dreams i run barefoot
down a street i've never seen.

in my waking life
i walk carefully,

ankles remembering
every twist.

my bedroom smells of vanilla
and rainwater.

a contradiction
i'm proud of.

i stand before the mirror,
trying on apologies
like dresses.

most hang loose,
some cut too deep,
none feel like mine.

i leave a little mascara
on his pillow
like a signature.

not on purpose.

not exactly.

i would have loved you right,
if you had just let me.

funny, how when i speak of beauty,
no one remembers my name-

like I was never part of picture i painted.

i loved you
like Icarus loved the sun—
too passionately
too horribly.

how little must i become,
if i am too much for you?

why can't i be sad

the person i love,
i don't love anymore.

she was another forest fire,
and the rain stopped her from being catastrophic.

i can't hear you and my demons at the same time—

but I still long for their whispers,
and trust you with my whole, breaking heart.

SHE

IS

LIAR.

she's an endless hall of mirrors;

every reflection is a disguise
for the single face she can't show.

she laughs louder
than she feels
so no one notices
how quietly her voice trembles

the truth inside her
isn't a pearl,
it's a blade
she keeps wrapped in cloth.

at night she pulls off
faces like petals,

and the last one left
can't even meet her own eyes.

call her liar
because her laughter is sewn
from scraps of other people's joy.

the face she wears
isn't hers but borrowed,
smoothed over the cracks
until it almost fits.

and beneath it all
beats a heart of stone—
not born of cruelty
but of kindness hardened,
because softness couldn't survive there.

so when she gives you a smile,
give one back.

it's the truest thing
she has left to offer.

with her borrowed teeth
she smiles.

she learned early

to speak like water
and feel like stone.

with a breath that tastes of smoke and old wine,

she moves like a secret
the world isn't ready to hear,

young enough to tempt, old enough to know.

she is a cheat, a liar,
her sins stitched on her sleeves,
each one a pulse,
each one alive.

if I sleep with someone else
and still think of you,
would you still let me in
without flinching at the truth?

she was never mine
i just kept hoping she would stay anyway.

i've buried my love in casket so many times
i no longer pretend to mourn it.

no matter the story she tells,
her eyes stay honest.

i breathe in the smoke to quickly
like I am trying to fill the emptiness before
it notices me.
maybe if I take enough short breaths,
god will mistake it for living and let me stay-

long enough for a thousand cigarettes to
graze my lips, because yours never will.

two halves of heart,
don't make two lovers.

a love that is shared— is a love called betrayal.

what if I told you that—

at first, healing is self destructive!!

The final one!!

i have walked through nights
that refused to speak,
and mornings that forgot my name.

these pages are the echoes
of everything I could not hold,
everything I could not say.

if you find yourself here,
leaning on these words,
know that you were never alone.

Author's Note

This book is a dream come true for me—my debut, long held on the shelf, waiting while fear whispered that I wasn't good enough. I don't fully know where the courage came from, or if it was simply an impulsive decision, but I am profoundly glad that I finally let it out into the world.

For years, these words lived quietly in notebooks, on scraps of paper, in the corners of my mind. I carried them like fragile fragments of myself, unsure if they were worthy of anyone's attention. And yet, here they are, breathing, alive, and ready to meet readers.

Writing this book taught me something I hope it teaches others too: that imperfection does not disqualify you, that vulnerability can be strength, and that sometimes, the scariest step— simply starting— is the most necessary.

This is my leap, my offering, and my hope: that in these pages, someone might see themselves, feel understood, or simply find a quiet companion in the words I dared to write.

If these words found you, follow the journey with me on my Instagram handle- @flumaer.

Share, write, or simply breathe them in—this book is as much yours as it is mine.

9 789334 412802

Printed at Repro India Ltd.